TALK TO ME

POETRY, PROSE, AND
PHOTOGRAPHY

ALEXI
LUBOMIRSKI

Andrews McMeel
PUBLISHING®

Other Books by Alexi Lubomirski

Princely Advice for a Happy Life

Thank You for My Dreams

For Giada, Sole Luka, and Leone.

INTRODUCTION

I was trapped.

I was, and still am, a fashion and portrait photographer, and I have been extraordinarily blessed in that field. The title of *photographer*, however, had become a self-inflicted restriction on my creativity. That is to say, that if and when I found myself inspired by something I saw, felt, or heard, I would automatically think of how to translate that into a photograph, little realizing how much that hindered the creative process.

Thankfully, several years ago, I recognized the limitations that I was placing on myself and made a decision to allow any form of creative inspiration to manifest itself into whatever medium served it best, be it poetry, prose, painting, or, of course, photography.

Once the shackles were removed, all creative hell broke loose. Memories, emotions, experiences, and reflections were funneled through my pen onto paper. Images of mine that held so much personal emotion and narrative in them were now able to be excavated and explored from an entirely different point of view. Added to this, the marriage of image and word was permitted, allowing photography to narrate poetry and vice versa.

Admittedly, the majority of my poetry is *for* and *about* my wife, Giada— which, for the time being, is for her eyes only. So, this collection of poetry is about everything and all else in between.

Alexi Lubomirski

CONTENTS

Share One Breath

Poems of Romance and Love

WHAT IS ROMANCE?

What does it mean to be *romantic*?
It is not a valentine's card or a red rose,
but the seed of thought behind those things.
For romance starts with love.

It is a way of life
that carries us through each day,
on far-reaching wings,
fueled by our wish to spread light.

It is helping someone reach higher.
It is lightening a stranger's load
or standing so they may sit.
It is seeing everyone with romance in our hearts.

For when we see life
through the romance of love,
we are able to live *with* love
and, therefore, give *through* love.

So let us smile at passersby
and give so others may prosper.
Let us think of others
with the care we afford our loved ones.

For this is *romance!*

It is offering a kind word of understanding,
even when rained upon by hate-filled arrows.
It is offering a helping hand,
when we have long ago spent our last bead of sweat.

This is *romance.*

When we are able to open our eyes
to the beauty and magic of life
and see others as our gods see them.
For they see us all as *their* children.

So I rise this morning,
with romance flowing from within.
Romance for the woman
with whom I share these lives,
romance for my sons,
for whom I wish to be the best of men,
and romance for this life
that will mirror my love,
for all of my days.

ALEXI LUBOMIRSKI

HOW SWEET THE IRONY.

How sweet the irony . . .
The one I love the most
is the one I get to photograph the least.

Maybe it is a blessing.
Like an addict who is denied his drug
lest he sink into a pool of obsession.

For it would be my obsession.
I could shoot her day and night
and never tire of her face or form.

As my eyes compose each frame,
my love and adoration
drink in every curve, angle, and gaze.

Instead of quenching my thirst,
each frame taken
just adds to the frenzied appetite for more.

Like a man possessed,
I want to step through the frame
and embrace this supernatural beauty.

You turn your head,
your eyes glance my way and pierce the lens,
and I am floored. . . .

I frantically press the shutter,
trying to catch that moment for eternity.
Desperately grasping at this transient vision.

With each image
I feel as though I am writing poetry,
trying to document in images the miracle I see before me.

The light that dances off your face
and the soft glow of your skin
are the similes and metaphors that form each verse.

I *write* as fast as I can with my shutter,
scared that I will miss a dip of your chin,
a raise of your eyebrow, a twinkle in your eye.

As fast as it began, it is over.
Life starts up again,
and I am left with whatever my camera has stolen.

Images that captured that incredible moment in time
when your eyes burnt a hole through a piece of glass
and pierced my soul.

Such is the sweet pain I feel.
To witness heaven's light for a brief second
before it disappears, once more, into the haze of life.

Thank God for my camera . . . and thank God for you.

YOU ARE BEAUTIFUL.

When you look in the mirror,
I hope you see what I see.

I see the glory of the world
and its intricate tapestry.

When you see yourself as different,
I see you as brilliantly unique.

Each curl, freckle, curve, and hue
are dazzling rays, shining from within you.

The shape of your eyes, color of your skin,
and texture of your hair
are the accents that define this radiance.

Your beauty is not only what you see in a photograph.
It is your smile, that mirrors your heart
and your warmth, that fills others with joy.

The same people who misunderstand your look today,
will be the same who laud it tomorrow.

So do not be swayed by their opinions of you.
They will change as often as the shifting winds.

Know in your heart that you are beautiful,
and that no one else has shone like you shine today.

THE WILL OF LOVE.

Dry musky air hits me like a charging bull
as I open the door onto the city walls.

The battle of Christian and Moor
continues high above the plain,
through songs of praise from each people,
gently echoing toward each other.

A lone man rides between them,
his silhouette disguising his allegiance.

What would it matter?
Each doctrine is just another face
of the same mountain, built on love.

How many sons and daughters have been killed?
How many homes torn apart?
How many dreams shattered?

This is not the will of love.

Love was meant to conquer all, not one another.

LOVE BE MY INHERITANCE.

The same water that melts from the mountaintop
will find its way down to the streams, rivers, and oceans.
In the same way that the blood my child carries
descends from the first of us, and thus to him.

Neither distance nor time can dilute
the very essence and strength of this flow.
We are but links in a glorious, proud chain
that binds us through each lifetime.

The eyes of each child
tell tales of many generations before.
Yet each resides in new vessels
that will carry us to new, undiscovered shores.

This is our journey!
This is our legacy!
Not in the material evidence that we accumulate,
but in the spiritual wake that shimmers behind us.

Love will be our inheritance,
honor, our estate!
Let all of our elders glow with pride,
safe in the knowledge that in each child lies our immortality.

THE EARLY BLUEBELL.

As I open the faded pages
of my old book of half-baked poems,
I see the flattened bluebell
that she gave me all those years ago.

She had tried in vain to explain
that our love was like that fragile flower.
She had picked it from the snow-covered ground,
explaining that it had bloomed too early.

My unwilling ears listened when she said
it had grown prematurely,
too eagerly, too soon, and thus would perish.
She told me that this was the way of such things.

I look at the pressed petals on the page.
The thin blue limbs, finer than tissue
and as delicate as a dew-covered web.
One touch and it would shrivel into dust.

Back then, I could not accept
that winter's icy hands
could not sustain this fragile love
until the temperate winds of spring.

Thus, here lie the remains of my unrequited love,
dormant between two chapters.
I place the relics on the table
and gently blow away the ashes of this love story's demise.

PURPOSE.

We enter this life with no possessions,
a simple, and yet complex, soul.
We have nothing, and we know nothing,
free from the shackles of our imminent lives.

Eventually, we will move on to the next plane,
and again we will leave with nothing.
Try as we might, we are unable to
carry any of our attained earthly riches.

All that we toiled for, all that we acquired,
will be for naught.
Our souls refusing to be weighed down
by these false gods.

So the question remains,
how can we leave this life
richer than when we arrived?
How do we enrich and therefore evolve our *souls?*

The answer floats in front of me,
easier to pluck from the air
than a low-hanging fruit
begging to be eaten.

Love.

That one simple word,
that cliché. That bumper sticker.
That word thrown about like confetti.
Yet, it is the answer . . . *love.*

To add infinite and immortal riches to our soul
and achieve some semblance of spiritual evolution,
all of our attempts have one simple, core ingredient.

Love.

The love that lies within charity.
The love that begins with chivalry.
The love that makes us stand up for others,
no matter their skin color or beliefs.

Then there is love for *all*.
Love for all the birds and beasts
that crawl, fly, and swim.
From the mighty whale, to the tiny bee.

Love for the life-giving forces of our world,
the jungles and oceans, deserts and mountains.
The powerful love that resonates when we choose
to protect the planet, which in turn protects us.

And then there is love of self.

By understanding that I am joined to the passerby,
the bee, the jungle,
this planet, and the energy that contains us all,
I begin to understand that *I am everything*.

So I sit in silence, and I choose to love myself.
In doing so, my love for I and *everything*
echoes in the people I meet, the actions I take,
the past, the present, and the future.

I decide to be rich. Richer than I could ever dream of.
Yet this will not be measured in coin, mortar, or land.
It will be counted in the lives that I touch,
the animals and environment I protect.

Love will be my mighty bow,
from which my life's purpose will be released.
I vow to love and therefore evolve.
This will be my inheritance.

WEDDING MORN.

Be still our racing hearts.
Your new chapter of love is opening its eyes.

Breathe . . . Feel the expectant air,
ripe with joy, magic, and blessings.

Calm . . . Be serene and enjoy each sense.
Feel the warm sun.
Hear the breeze whisper in your ear that you are loved.

See the space between each moment
and slowly taste the birth of love.

Walk among friends and loved ones.
Absorb each word, each hug, each kiss.

Sup from this affection until you are full . . .
and then love, love, love.

SHE GIVES.

As the sun gives warmth and light,
with no agenda
other than to see happiness
reflected on the recipient's face,
so, too, does this woman's love help others
to scale their own personal mountains.

With a smile that sheds light
on any shadow
and a grace that disguises
the power of her reach,
time after time she continues to step in
and help me shine my own little light.

So as I offer thanks to the sun
for its unselfish gifts,
I also give thanks to her
for her unwavering warmth, light, and love
that she shares daily with myself and others.

A KISS.

Every day we share a kiss.
A *Good morning* kiss,
a *Hello* kiss,
an *I love you* kiss.

Kids run around,
meals get made.
We rush from daily routine to daily routine.
A kiss here, a kiss there. *I love you . . . I love you, too.*

A week passes.
Two weeks pass.
I love you. Kiss kiss.
We work, we laugh, we sleep.

Stop.

When is a kiss, a kiss?
For once, let us stay still
for longer than the time it takes
to touch lips and smile.

We need to stop and look at each other.
We need to lock eyes
for more than a fleeting glance
between kids and life.

Lean forward.

Share one breath.
Nose to nose,
we are close enough to see into each other.
I remember you, before all of this happened.

You are *her*.
You are that girl who woke my heart
from a deep slumber.
You are the girl I kissed at a party.

You are the one who roused my capacity to love,
the soul that called mine into the open.
The beauty that inspired and inspires me still.
The mother of our beautiful boys.

Now lean further still.

I gently touch your full lips.
Again I move closer.
Lips part, tongues lightly caress,
I feel that fizz that I felt the first time.

This is my girl.
The girl whose real kiss
makes me *feel* love.
The spirit whom my heart belongs to.

Again and again we kiss.
My top lip feels ripe and fizzes once more.
Still touching, we smile at each other.
How I love those smiling eyes.

The world around us
that for a moment had paused
starts to speed up again.
"Mummy! Daddy! Can I have a . . ."

We dive back into the daily river of duty,
love remembered and renewed.
As we get pulled in opposite directions,
I look over at you.

I love you, I say

I know . . .

Born of Love

Poems of Family and Fatherhood

I WRITE FOR THE FATHER.

I write for the father,
on the road far away,
sacrificing sacred shared time
to provide for his young.

I write for the father,
severed by divorce,
forced to spend dreaded holidays
with only his pain-drenched thoughts for company.

I write for the father,
working three jobs that he hates,
to give his children a stronger start
than he himself inherited.

I write for the father,
crawling on work-weary knees,
to build train sets, tea parties,
and Lego-lined memories.

I write for the father,
fighting to balance time
between work, wife, and kids,
never winning or surrendering.

I write for the father,
sitting by a hospital bed,
declining sleep or rest,
lest his daughter wake and call for him.

I write for the father,
taking a needed deep breath,
fighting back screams of frustration
as he cradles an inconsolable child.

I write for the father,
falling asleep on his son's bed
in work clothes,
Goodnight Moon, open on his chest.

I write for the father,
who declines that post-work beer
in favor of returning home
to take over bath time.

I write for the father,
attempting to connect with his daughter
as she explains her life choices
that he reluctantly accepts.

I write for the father,
curled up in his child's crib,
providing comfort and care
for his terminally ill girl.

I write for the father,
instilling values in his son,
to treat all people with respect
no matter their skin color or creed.

I write for the father,
stuck in his bigoted ways,
who instinctively embraces his son
when he fearfully comes out to his parents.

I write for the father,
battling with a volcanic rage,
weeping behind closed doors
after screaming at his child.

I write for the father,
childhood tainted with abuse and pain,
who now struggles
not to let history repeat itself.

I write for the father,
cradling his newborn as she sleeps,
vowing to love without measure
and be all that she needs.

I write for the father,
of children with dark skin,
who knows of this world's prejudice
and the injustice that still exists.

I write for the single father,
taking on both parents' roles,
being stretched in all directions
as daily life leaves him ravaged.

I write for the man,
whose children death has stolen too soon,
who refuses to surrender
his title of *Father*.

I write for the father,
nursing his daughter's broken heart again
knowing full well *that* boy
will be in her arms again soon.

I write for the father,
unjustly behind bars,
missing his children grow
and unable to heal the pain of his absence.

I write for the father,
estranged from his children,
wondering if tomorrow will be too late
to swallow his pride and reach out.

And I write for the father,
taking his last breath of this life,
with his children's love
surrounding him
as they thank him for being their *dad*.

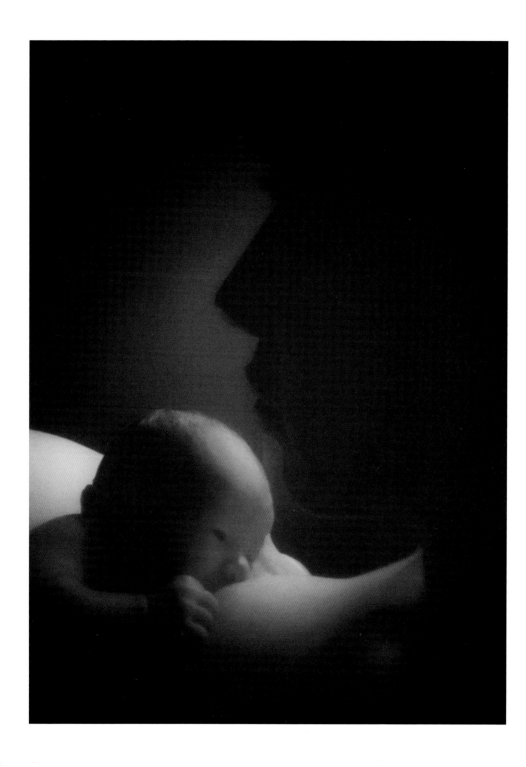

ALEXI LUBOMIRSKI

MAMA.

I loved you before I knew what love was.
The curve of your smiling eye
and your warm embrace
were all the world I needed to know.

As I grew, year after year,
I felt your love in every fiber of my being.
I felt happy when you were happy, sad when you were sad,
such was the strength of our bond.

As an adolescent, I made the customary mistakes.
I rejected you to prove my independence,
and in the process, hurt the only love
that would be there no matter what.

I yearned for your approval, even when pretending not to.
A proud smile made my confidence soar,
and a disapproving eye left me crushed inside
because to me, you are everything.

My love for you deepened
after the birth of my sons,
as I finally understood what you always felt
and do feel, to this day.

We have both aged now,
and I have evolved from protectee to protector.
As we outgrew you, my siblings and I
began to discuss your well-being, more than our own.

But still you remain my guardian,
and despite your smaller frame,
you will always represent the Atlas
who supports the roof of the world above my head.

Now allow us to lighten *your* burden,
knowing that you have set us on our paths.
Rest now and enjoy the love that surrounds you,
now and forever.

BORN OF LOVE.

You are my son, born of love.
I see in your eyes all the nations and bloods that comprise you,
drawing from many soils, lands, and coasts.
In you lies the very best of me, all that is good that I have to offer.

Cradling you in my arms, I gaze upon a life yet unknown.
Stand, then, on my shoulders and scale the heavens!
Take from me all that is honorable, all that is noble and true,
leaving behind any malice or malcontent.

Watching you grow is life's single greatest pleasure.
Each new step, each new word, lifts my heart and brings light into my world.
May God grant me the courage to release you from my arms,
safe in the knowledge that I have guided you fair and true.

Let my arms grant you protection;
let my love teach you compassion;
let my actions guide your character;
let my words give you wisdom.

You are Love. You are loved. You are my son.

BEST FRIENDS.

Days are whiled away musing on life,
love, and what tomorrow may bring.

We occasionally marvel at the wind and the passing clouds.
We listen for the faint hum of distant airplanes,
while staring in wonder at beads of water
dancing delicately on morning leaves.

Laughing in unison,
we sigh into a comfortable silence,
knowing each other
as only we do.

A running race,
a hand-cupped face.
Each moment side by side
rings with divine blessings.

I see that he has no concerns,
no fears, and no insecurities.
He inspires me to live in the present,
to enjoy *now* and to be *here*.

He has a peace that I envy.
Yet I know that
as he educates me now,
so will I repay him one day.

My first waking thought is of him.
Is he awake? What is he doing?
What adventures will we share today?
Will we laugh so hard that no sound emits?
Will we speak volumes with just one look?

Such a short lifetime
together
and we are alike
in so many ways.
He and I are young in body and spirit, respectively.
Naïve enough together to have no burdens,
no ego, and no agendas.
We simply *exist* when side by side.

I pray this golden union
stands strong forever.
This boy is my best friend.
This boy is my infant son.

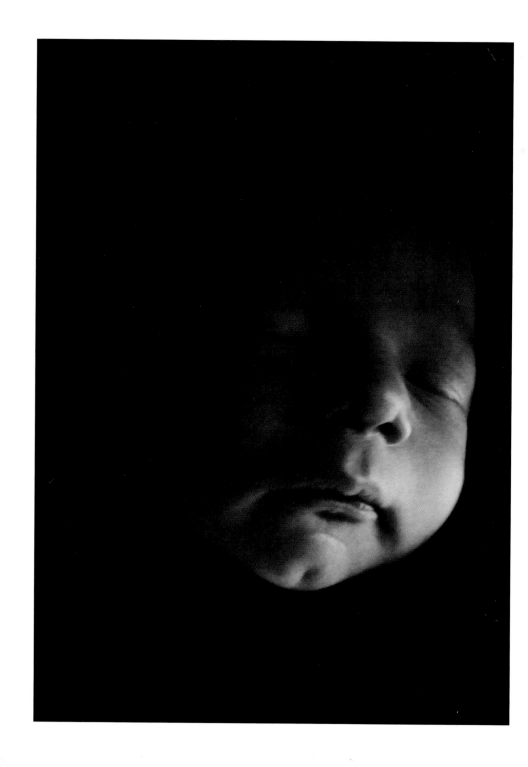

BIRTH.

A twenty-foot wave of energy,
saturated with life, full of love,
has just driven through my chest,
leaving me wordless and gasping for air.

It was not a surprise.
I have seen him growing
within your radiant and ripe womb
for the last two hundred and eighty days.

However, I could not *feel* him as you could.
I could not connect
on that physical and emotional plane,
as you have done through blood and sinew.

I have whispered fatherly nothings
through your stretched skin,
and I have sung him the classics.
But that was akin to talking through a brick wall.

You have felt him grow.
You have fed and protected him.
He rises with your joy and tenses with your pain,
and thus you are forever bonded in love.

Yet I have waited on the side
like a substitute player,
wanting to help and be of service.
Love, excitement, and fear bubbling just below the surface.

As we raced to the hospital
through New York City's dead of night,
things started to lean toward surrealism,
and I assumed a leading role in the movie of this night.

Still your belly is swollen and glowing.
Still I lend my inconsequential support.
Still I follow in blind faith,
believing that a baby will indeed enter our world soon.

One final push!
One final push!
An almighty life-defining scream,
and the doctor lifts up his arms.

My world falls silent.
I am left floating in a vacuum of light and sounds
as I raise my eyes to bear witness
to his arrival: *My son.*

The cosmos catches up
with this black hole in time,
and a thunderous bolt pierces my chest,
leaving me struck down by Love's sword.

This being whom I will know forever.
This child who is the sum of our deepest love.
This . . . this person,
whom I will lay down my life for.

Thank you! My God, thank you!

I WOULD HAVE BEEN YOUR FRIEND.

If I was not your father in this lifetime,
I would like to have been your friend.
How I would love to be the same age as you,
to play and experience life for the first time together.

I would admire your kind and gentle spirit,
your genuine empathy for others,
and your eagerness to protect our Earth Mother,
joined with your constant, open nature.

I would gravitate toward your easy laughter,
your generous smile,
and the light in your eyes;
your name being the perfect fit for your character.

Your beautiful spirit and tender soul
have no agenda or fear.
Your welcome is real,
and your warmth is from the heart.

I would love to share a friendship with that person.
To laugh and grow together as kindred spirits.
I would feel blessed to have such a comrade
whose outlook has such positivity and love.

There is an unspoken sadness of parenting,
for when the children eventually reach adulthood,
the parent will have since graduated to old age.
We can never share the same time together.

I will therefore watch as you grow
and be happy for your friends.
I know how lucky they are,
and I smile at how lucky I am to be your father.

SWIMMING WITH SONS.

As the water envelops me,
I feel instantly cleansed;
my soul being purified
from the noise of daily life.

I glide forward
into the water's depths.
The silent, liquid cocoon
reminding me of a womb-like comfort.

I surface and open my eyes into the light.
Shrieks of joy explode into the silence
as four arms lasso themselves around my neck,
and two faces press against mine.

"Look at me! Look what I can do!"
"Well done! Amazing! When did you get so strong?!"
For hours, we feed off each other's giddy exhilaration,
drenched in love with the moment and with each other.

Between jumps,
splashes, and laughter,
there are calmer moments of hugs,
kisses, and just *being* together.

Both sons' arms are crisscrossed around my neck
like a winter scarf,
and I feel the sensation of two tiny hearts,
beating excitedly against my body.

These are the moments
that I will always remember.
No photograph or video
could ever fully describe this depth of joy.

I force myself to stop and savor
this delicate, delicious moment.
I hug them a little closer, kiss their foreheads,
and tell them of my love for them.

I tell them to breathe deeply,
to notice the jet-blue sky and the lush, green trees,
to listen to the warm wind
that scatters itself through the leafy canopy above.

I tell them how fortunate we are
to have this moment,
and I teach them how to give thanks for the sky,
the sun, and their blessings.

As quickly as the moment of stillness arrived, it is gone,
and the chaos of two young boys begins once more.
Each jump is bigger, each breath held longer,
and my pride swells further.

Utter joy permeates my body,
knowing I am teaching them something,
that has given me such pleasure
throughout my life.

Exhausted and spent,
we clamber out of the water,
and we wrap the young in towels
like gifts under a tree.

With only their eyes peering out,
they curl up in their mother's arms
and excitedly tell her tales
of their watery adventures.

I lazily slink back into the warm water
and submerge myself.
Releasing all air from my lungs,
I sink to the bottom.

I lie in silence looking up at the fallen leaves
floating on the surface
that break up the low rays
of the late afternoon sun.

As the air
in my body diminishes,
I am acutely aware of the emotions
I feel because of my sons.

They teach me how to be present,
how to live in and love the moment.
With no agenda,
they share their love and joy with me.

As the last of the air
escapes my body,
the happiness in my chest
floats me skyward.

"Daddy catch me!"

BROTHERS.

I look up, and I suddenly see you both a little older.
I try to make sense of my emotions
as I watch you together on top of the hill.
I feel my heart brimming with pride and love.

From time to time, I notice you both with fresh eyes,
and I wonder who you are and where you came from.
Did you come from me? Am I an adult? A father?
Who are these personalities forming in front of me?

You both possess such empathy and compassion.
I can only hope that I nurture what is in your hearts,
remembering that you are not mine to *lead*.
Instead, you are mine to *guide.*

You are not here to right my wrongs or fulfill my wishes.
You are here to become who *you* were meant to be.
I am but a caring and loving arm
if you need support along the way.

It is perhaps a blessing that you will never understand
a parent's love until you become one.
For if you knew, the knowledge might be too heavy a burden
and could steer you from your true destiny due to the guilt it can inflict.

A parent's love is something that no one prepares you for.
It can lift you to the mountaintops and drop you to your knees in seconds.
One can neither overcome it nor beat it down
as my happiness lies happily in that of yours.

COMING-OF-AGE PREVIEW.

I see the preview for your coming-of-age story,
and I am filled with love, dread, and hope.
For as I climbed and fell through my adolescence,
now, so must you.

You are but eight and she only ten,
and I feel myself torn
between wanting to protect your heart
and envying the beautiful pain of young love yet to come.

Will she outgrow you when she reaches teen-hood
and spurn you in favor of older boys?
Will you then catch up in later years
and win back the eye of that young, Italian summer love?

The sweet innocence
that I see in the eyes of you both,
carries neither hidden motive nor wicked games.
Just pure unsullied joy of being together.

I can only love you
and be here when you need,
praying that you are not wounded too greatly
in the many skirmishes of love that lie before you.

So enjoy this moment!
Bathe in this naïve love,
where tomorrow does not exist
and yesterday is all but forgotten.

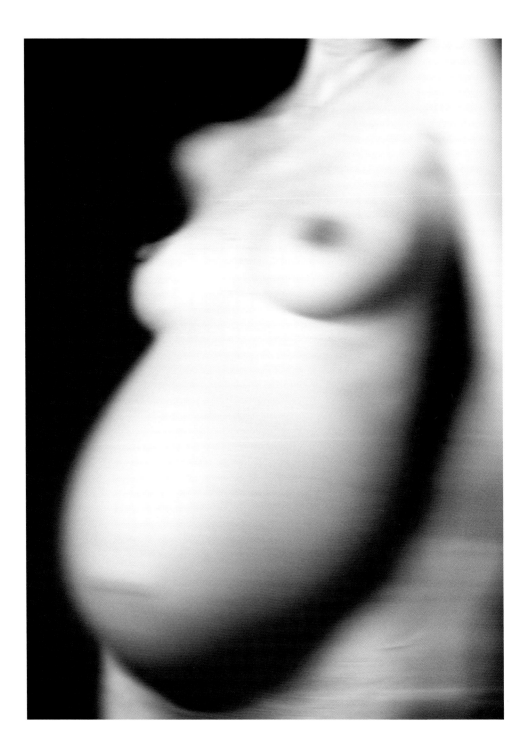

MOTHER GUIDE.

I am a stranger to all but you.
You, who knows every fiber
in the fabric of my being.
Each stitch, each frayed edge, each tear.

Every meteoric rise and catastrophic fall
has been witnessed, heard, and guided by you.
You remain the one constant in my life
that has never faltered or failed.

As sure as the sun replaces the moon,
you are there to shed a lone guiding light,
ready to play listener, offer a shoulder, or play oracle
depending on the need.

For only a mother can comprehend
the complexities of all present
and past life chapters
that have directed, shaped,
and created her child.

And for this I am grateful.

THE CHILDREN.

Whether we know it or not,
we place an oppressive pressure on our children.
Simply wanting them to be happy
places a burden on their very being.

For their existence is an extension of us,
a postponed chance to find the unknown.
We want them to be happy,
for that will, in turn, bring *us* happiness.

They carry within them *our* hope.

We fear that we will not accomplish
everything we wish to.
We fear we may not succeed
and evolve spiritually as we had once hoped.

Goals that move
beyond our reach.
Personality traits that we are
unable to push through.

On our children, we unwittingly place
our second chance for fulfillment.
We wish them to better us.
We will them to rise where we fell.

We inadvertently expect their achievements
to pull *us* over the finish line.

We blind ourselves to their own mountain climbs.
Just as we have dharmas,
they have theirs to fulfill.

So let us release them
from the storied weight of our ambitions
and watch them blossom uninhibited
into that which they need to become.

TODAY I LOST A PARENT.

I watch my infant son in the playground,
as he dares himself further.
Further still, he ventures from me,
frequently looking back to confirm my status.

I sense his courage and pride
as well as his comfort
in knowing that I am but yards away,
lest fear or failure befall him.

Today I lost a parent,
and I feel myself as a child
bravely venturing into the world,
safe in the knowledge that a parent looked over me.

Except this time, I look back
over the playground of my life,
and I see no one.
I feel alone and untethered.

No matter how far I have traveled,
the countries and oceans crossed,
I always felt the security
of my distant parent, lest I fell.

Even into my fourth decade,
I unknowingly retained that infantile comfort
of stretching myself further
and looking back for their loving approval.

But today I am a boat set adrift
alone on an ocean, far from whence I came.
The lighthouse of my home,
snuffed out, never to be rekindled.

One of the mighty pillars
that held the world's roof atop my head
has crumbled and fallen,
passing their Atlasian duty to me.

A sudden realization arises
that adulthood has landed at my feet,
and I am now the safety net
for the next generation.

I will now be that beacon
shining from the home shores of my young,
offering them a proud and comforting glow,
until the day that I will have to pass my loving torch to them.

SMOKING WITH JOHN.

I can still smell the pungent aroma
of his Silk Cut tobacco
that hovered in the dusty evening heat
on our small Botswanan back porch.

He would request my presence after dinner,
as he sucked on the burning embers
of his smoky digestif,
and I begrudgingly followed, his whiskey in hand.

I was eight, or nine, or maybe ten,
and unaware of the significance of those moments.
Those treasured evening episodes
when I stood awkwardly by his side.

He would inhale deeply,
puffing his cheeks out
as the smoke circled within,
before exhaling the exhausted residues.

I watched the snaking haze
as it rose up to the solitary, flickering bulb,
momentarily clearing a path
through the throng of winged light disciples.

Two puffs in, and he would break the silence
as he pointed out a passing satellite.
Lining up my eye to his arm,
I followed his knuckled finger to the stars above.

A small, insignificant flashing light
crawled slowly across the skies,
following a pin-straight course,
and my imagination was launched into the heavens.

I felt infinitesimal
as I imagined what this orbiting voyeur
was watching below its bow,
and I leaned my head against the pocketed arm to my left.

Our eyes stared skyward,
lost in the millions of galaxies above,
waiting for any sudden movement or sign,
with only the occasional waft of smoke blurring our view.

Suddenly, entering on stage left,
a blaze of light shot across the skies.
"There's one!" he exclaimed with childlike glee,
at our first shooting star of the night.

And so it would continue,
this celestial performance,
crowned with the nocturnal soundtrack
of bird, beast, and insect, for an audience of two.

The spent cigarette butt,
sucked in on itself and stained yellow,
was flicked into the darkness beyond
as he ruffled my hair, signifying the end of our interlude.

And that was it.
We would walk through the swing door,
and I would catch the tail end of some vapid '80s TV show
as he recounted news from the day's work to my mother.

How I would pay to spend one more evening
below the stars with him.
I would hold his hand in mine,
memorizing every word, inhaling every moment.

So now I sit, a solitary grown man,
with the spirit of my stepfather on my left.
I converse with him about the sounds and the stars.
And we smile. And we laugh. And we exist.

Hallowed Land, Holy Land

Poems of Nature and Environment

HALLOWED LAND, HOLY LAND.

Hallowed land, holy land.
Sacred land, stolen land.
Where cactus, bird, and dragonfly
are as one.

This land is your land,
This land is my land . . .
floats through the rocks
like a poisonous echo over scorched earth.

Celebrating days of discovery
and of thanks and of giving
by feasting and amassing,
further rubbing salt into their Wounded Knee.

We stomp across this land
crushing unseen holy relics under wheel and track,
never stopping to learn, witness, or comprehend
our connection to the basic elements.

We cannot read the wind
nor converse with the light.
The silent whisper of the desert's morning dew
cannot be heard over our Instagram life.

Our detachment is wider than
the ocean that once separated us.
In lieu of the earth, stars, and sun,
we bow our heads to overfiltered false gods.

We are unable to right the wrongs
done to the first people of this land,
so deeply plunged into their hearts
is our venom-stained dagger.

But hope is not all drained
from the dry riverbeds of this valley.
Its delicate balance floats on the eagle's wing
and rests within each rock and tree.

Let us halt this maddening advance
and open our hearts to our bonded existence
with this land and its treasured wisdom
that will exist long after our last footprint
is blown from the sand.

VEGAN POEM.

Something woke me up . . .
A split-second occurrence
that led me from *there* to *here*
and now, thank God, I cannot return.

Like an ex-smoker cleaning an ashtray,
an ex-drinker surrounded by slurred conversation,
an ex-addict being shouted at by his friends.
Once we move on, it pains us to see what we once were.

Now the fog has lifted, I truly see the sentient creatures around me.
I see them as I see my family.
I see them as fathers, mothers, and companions.
And I see how eerily numb I was.

How could I have been blind to what I now understand?
Today, I realize that everything I believed
was programmed into me from birth.
I could not have known, because I was taught not to.

Why would I *want* to know anyway?
There was a happy clown serving a burger,
a laughing cow, bright colors and smiling faces.
Why would these images lie to me?

I ignored the voice in my head and heart
that screamed at me to wake up from this lunacy.
I turned the other way when I was shown the truth,
favoring, instead, that delicious and blissful ignorance.

But now I am awake!

Now the door has been pushed open,
the light is bursting through,
and there is no more stopping the tide.
Inspiration, thoughts, and realizations will not be ignored.

The voice in my heart and head is no longer silenced.
Instead it has the floor, and it *will* be heard!
Bit by bit, alterations are made.
One by one, minds are changed.

No more numbness to the truth.
No more killing my brothers and sisters.
No more making excuses.
It is time for us to evolve.

FALL FIRESTORM.

The crunch of fall underfoot
is the only sound I hear,
as I stand among the half-dressed trees
partly devoid of their summer fashions.

The summer wind that sang lullabies to me
through the leafy branches of July,
now slips unencumbered
through cold, wooden fingers, creaking above.

The musky scent of our home's fireplace
rolls gently off the roof and dissipates around us,
bringing with it a sense of comfort
and warmth and family and love.

The misty, damp hue
that hovers above the land
sucks all life from every palette
of leaf, plant, and beast.

A sudden exhale of wind
flusters clouds that quickly break formation.
Then one, two, maybe four spears of sunlight
slice through the gray canopy.

As if God himself, sitting on high,
had ordered a bombing raid upon the earth,
explosion after explosion of electrified color
bursts from tree to unassuming tree.

Crimson flames follow yellow fireballs
as God's wrath tears across the valley,
detonating each tree in its path.
The land igniting like Pompeii against a backdrop of slate gray.

But the clouds are not beaten yet.
They regroup and prepare a counterattack.
Circling back around, they close in on Zeus's thunderbolts,
and with each ambush, the light is snuffed out.

Again, I find myself standing in silence
cloaked within a desaturated landscape.
Energized by the brief monsoon of color,
I head in to warm myself by our home's humble inferno.

THE ROCK.

How many hands
have been placed
on this mighty rock?

How many tears
of joy and sorrow
have been shed beside it?

How many oaths sworn,
brothers bonded,
or loves declared?

This ancient stone,
weathered by wars,
for which blood
has been spilt and battles fought.

This unmovable beast
whose monk-like silence
holds the stories
of mortal men.

It cares not for money or land,
religion or power.
But what of love?
Does it *feel* as we do?

If *it* and *we* are but different fruits
grown from the same tree, born of stardust,
do we not then feel the same longing,
the same fulfillment or anguish?

Can we not therefore
connect on some deeper level,
some common ground
that is at the base of all energy?

A rock is of the earth,
and the earth feeds the tree,
which then feeds man and womankind.
So how, then, can we deny our bond?

Man's arrogance tells us
that we have dominion over this rock,
but we are as inconsequential
to it as an ant is to man.

It will spectate over millennia,
as great dynasties rise and fall,
with the same interest
as we give one day changing to the next.

CLEANING BEACHES.

I have cleaned beaches before
with my wife and sons.
We have made it fun,
and we have made it educational.

But today was the first time
that I did it alone,
and I felt ashamed, helpless,
and angry at myself.

I felt the stares of sunbathers around me.
Those bemused faces that I had seen before
every time they watched my wife
picking up straws and cigarette butts around them.

Their faces revealed confusion,
shame, and sometimes anger.
Anger at the way it made them feel.
Anger that the problem was exposed.

We are on holiday, they tell me with their eyes.
They don't want to feel guilty.
You shouldn't make us feel this way, he says
by pushing his cigarette into the sand next to his towel.

I carry on undeterred. The more I pick up, the more I see,
and I am further motivated to find it all.
I realize painfully how blind we all are
to the unstoppable, polluted wake we leave behind us.

And I am angry. Angry at myself for the years of neglect.
Angry at the corporations too big to care.
Angry at us all for thinking it is not our problem.
Angry that it is almost, if not already, too late.

My five-year-old son joins me,
and his words are positive
in spite of what he is picking up from the sand around him.
And I see hope in him.

Hope that people are waking up.
Hope that the old order is being replaced.
Hope that maybe we can make a change, in time.
Hope that we are not blind to our own demise.

"This is how we say 'Thank you' to the beach," my son says,
and I smile,
vowing to show my gratitude
to each and every beach from here on. . . .

CAVE OF WONDERS.

I rise before the light
and venture out
onto the barren land,
bathed in a blue-gray wash.

The ground faintly cracks
under my first, cautious step.
Above my head, each twig and seed
is encased in its own icy chrysalis.

A land snared
in winter's spell,
waiting for spring's thaw
to release it from its icy tomb.

The north wind blows through
the tree's frigid fingers,
cracking them like the knuckles
of Old Man Winter himself.

A shaft of light breaks free
and illuminates the snow beneath me,
as the sun crests the frozen horizon,
revealing a terrain littered with precious stones of ice.

In an instant, this dawn's radiance
enlightens each bud, leaf, and branch;
their glassy cocoons exploding with light
in diamond-like majesty.

The land before me transforms
from a lifeless graveyard
to a cave of wonders,
with a thousand decadent chandeliers vying for attention.

I am left mesmerized and entranced
by nature's transient yet glorious treasures,
giving thanks
for her daily unexpected gifts.

SOMETHING GREATER.

I am the conscious young girl,
requesting no meat,
regardless of the taunts of her brother
and the deaf ears of her parents.

I am the young man,
facing rejection
from his teammates and friends
for politely refusing that burger.

I am the concerned mother
who wants to stop ignoring the truth
and start feeding meat alternatives to her children,
but who is shamed by her peers.

I am the husband
who is seen by his wife
as less masculine
because he won't eat red meat anymore.

I am the few
who stand tall for our beliefs,
withstanding the jeers,
the insults, and indifference of others.

I am those who choose to lead with the few,
in spite of the many.
I am the proud who gains strength
from every negative slight sent my way.

So let them sneer when they feel awkward.
Let them attack that which they do not understand.
I will sup courage from their disdain
and be emboldened by their apathy.

For I stand for something larger
and will not condemn those who do not stand with me.
For I stand for them all
until they choose to stand by themselves.

LATE LIFE CHOICES.

It is hard to hear a critique of one's life choices.
To discover that we have been driving in the wrong direction
for hundreds of miles
and that our daily comforts create daily harm for others.

Late in life, late in the game,
we are presented with an unnerving decision.
Do we continue on the path of tradition,
despite our heart's realization that there lies a better way?

Our other choice is full of fear and the unknown.
For we are asking ourselves to uproot
everything that we toiled and labored to obtain,
all that we were taught to acquire.

We hear daily shouts of,
"Recycle! Compost! Organic! Vegan!
Sustainable! No Plastic!"
And so on and so on.

"I am too old to change!"
Am I too old to change?
Do I still not have the strength of will
and the freedom to improve my life and that of those around me?

Will I spend the latter half of my life
bitterly defending my choices in these modern times,
or will I open my wings to the winds of change
and renew myself many more times before my chips run out?

Will I lead by example
and change the hearts and minds of others like me?
Will I stand proud as others scoff at the new me?
What will my legacy be to me and those I love?

I am not in a box yet!

I can do more good in my remaining years
than I ever did in my past.
I will not be ashamed of what I have been
but *I will* be proud of what I will become!

LET US LIE SILENT.

Stop! Let us lie silent for just one second
and listen to the serenade
of the water dancing with the pebble.

Let us sing to the wind
that brings hope and light
from across the horizon.

Let us marvel at the insects
gathering sustenance
between flower and earth.

Let us sway peacefully
as we watch the maple tree
reciting the dawn chorus to the waning moon.

Let us press our ears
to these mighty rocks
and hear their chaptered stories of this land.

Let us gaze at the eagles' wings
as they are lifted
by the gentle whispers of each hill.

Let us give thanks
for the generosity of this land
before we are gone and returned to its creator.

FOUR DOORWAYS.

When asked
why one should turn
to a diet of compassion,
I offer doorways, four.

For love of all living beings.
Listen to your heart,
to the bloodied stories screaming to be heard
behind our innocently named meals.

To be able to align
our true heart's belief
with our daily wish
to survive and thrive.

For love of the environment.
Leave behind
our old, unbalanced, misguided ways
and start nurturing our Earth, as it has us.

To close the torture camps,
which in turn
brutalize the surrounding
air and earth and stream.

For love of our health.
Cease to ingest
the pain, sorrow, and fear
that course through the veins of each doomed beast and fowl.

Allow yourself to feed
off the living plants of this land
rather than partaking
in the premeditated murder of the killing fields.

For love of spiritual evolution.
Step toward enlightenment,
which then engulfs us,
opening our reservoirs of compassion.

Through compassion, comes understanding.
Through understanding, comes connection.
Only then can we bridge the void
betwixt our ill-informed wishes and our soul's true desire.

We select a door,
wondering if we chose wisely.
Yet the universal source of all rewards love and courage
with prizes behind all doors.

No matter the initial intention,
we reap the benefits
and are granted the seeds
to benefit all others.

We save our fellow creatures.
We bless our bodies with health.
We return love to our Earth
and open our hearts to a deeper evolving of the soul.

Live Not with Fear

Poems of Hope and Inspiration

I DREAM OF A YOUNGER ME.

This last night, I dreamed of my fifteen-year-old self.
A distant memory that came flooding back,
with all the clarity of color and sound
as if it were today.

I am sitting in the center
of a feebly executed crop circle,
my tame attempt at rebellion,
and I stew in a teenager's cauldron of insecurity and fear.

From my jean pocket, I take out my father's box of matches
and try to light a pocket-flattened joint.
The unceasing westerly wind flowing across this field
hampers my efforts, leaving me painfully alone with my thoughts.

I lift my gaze over the dusk-painted sky
and wish to be different, or older, or cooler.
I make a vow to myself that night,
that one far-off day, I will remember this moment, and I will smile.

One day I will be doing that which I love.
One day I will be living in a fast-paced city,
far away from this empty field and my adolescent contemplations.
One day I will have shed this confused, half-formed persona.

I will have finally felt the tenderness
of a girl's lust-filled lips,
and maybe even known the quiet ecstasy
of making love to a beautiful woman.

I will be married to a mysterious beauty
from across the oceans,
who would not know me
as this angst-ridden youth.

I will be at peace with whom I have become.
All my perceived shortcomings
will be considered strengths to draw from.
No longer a sheep following the flock, but a lone lion boldly advancing.

My eyes suddenly blink open,
and I find myself straddling two worlds.
My memorial emotions and senses reacting to the past
and my physical self, lying here in the present.

I turn and see my Cuban Italian love
sleeping beside me, in my New York home,
and I remember that young version of myself,
and I smile. . . .

INSPIRATION IN WAVES.

There are days when I see inspiration everywhere,
when imagery and words crash through my mind in mighty waves.
When everything I see, taste, or hear
is alchemized into the genesis of a new thought process.

Days when I am innately in tune
with every fiber of my being and surroundings.
Every emotion and every sense
channels perfectly through to my artistic muscle.

Like a world-class athlete,
all pistons fire in every distant corner of my imagination,
and I am merely a funnel
for each exhalation of the creative consciousness.

Every word follows the last, from I know not where.
Every angle or choice of color comes more naturally than breathing.
My creativity merely repeats ideas as they are plucked from the ether,
and my body obeys, moving in perfect symmetry.

I feel unstoppable, grateful, and elated all at once,
knowing that at this exact moment, everything is aligned.
The inner and the outer and everything in between is at my fingertips,
and I thankfully harvest for as long as I am allowed.

And then there are the other days.

Those days when I feel as if I am pushing a train over gravel.
No matter how hard I pray or try to force divine inspiration,
there is nothing but ash hanging in the surrounding air.
I taste the despair of the creative void.

I sit with pen in hand and try to create momentum
and encourage some inspiration to form.
But then I realize it is not mine to manifest.
It is just some otherworldly gift that I am lucky enough to receive.

It comes from somewhere above and below us,
somewhere within and without.
It is a simple, incredible, and wondrous gift
that comes at the best and worst of times.

So I continue to prepare and work on my foundation.
I meditate, staying clear, present, and aware,
creatively feeding myself whenever possible,
equipped with gratitude for the next mighty wave to roll in.

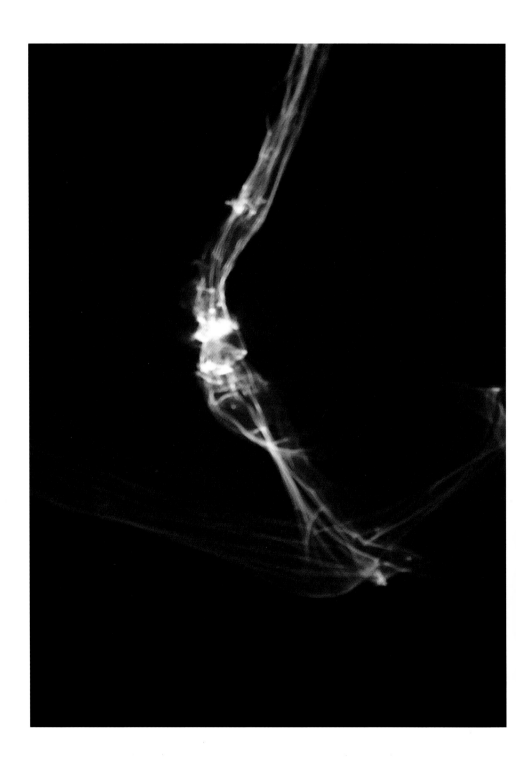

MY INK RUNS DRY.

My ink runs as dry
as a drought-stricken stream
that once fed a valley
and now gives birth to naught but dust.

Still my pen hovers,
my thumb clicking the pen top,
hoping that the next click
will ignite the flame of inspiration.

Nothing . . .
The clouds are devoid of sustenance,
The orchards stand fruitless.
My land is barren.

Still the pen hovers,
awaiting some divine being to descend from on high,
wield my pen betwixt finger and thumb
and chisel metaphor after golden metaphor on to paper.

Nothing. Nada.
The sea? The stars? My love for her?
I feel myself sinking into a creative chasm,
frantically grasping at any seedling of an idea.

I close my book and reopen it,
trying to fool myself into a fresh start,
but I see nothing but the unimpressed lines of the page,
looking at me like a dissatisfied lover.

"This has never happened before," I exclaim through deceitful lips
as I force my limp pen to paper.
Write *something,* I pathetically plead,
looking skyward for any drop of inspiration.

I resign myself to writing *anything* that enters my head,
not caring if it is just one random word
followed by another.
Just write something, for God's sake! . . . And then I write.

"My ink runs as dry
as a drought-stricken stream . . ."

MISS PHOTO FRAME.

At 6 p.m. sharp every Friday,
she would knock on my grandfather's door.
In her hand she carried a suitcase full of framed pictures
from which she would choose one or two.

My grandfather was the only person in the building
who had a camera or knew how to properly use one.
They had met on the corner of Mott and Spring
when she returned from her shift at the department store.

The first time she came to his room,
we hardly recognized her.
She was a different person
from that tattered, bruised girl on the street.

She couldn't have been older than twenty,
and even though she rarely muttered a word to either of us,
I fell immediately in love with her,
despite my younger years.

Dressed as if she were going to the finest church,
she waited for my grandfather to move the sofa
and put up the colored paper backdrop.
Then she would choose a picture and pose with it.

Some days it was a picture of children.
Other days it would be an old man or a young woman.
Were these her children, her husband, her siblings?
There was never any explanation or any emotion shown.

She came in for a total of eight months,
the greatest eight months of my adolescent life.
On each visit, she would collect the last week's photo,
put it into a stamped envelope in her bag, and leave without a word.

After she stopped coming in
and after much interrogation,
my grandfather finally told me
she was an orphan from the war.

Owning nothing,
she borrowed clothes from the store at night
and dressed herself like the mannequins in the window,
to be photographed.

"And the photos?" I asked,
"Were they real?"
"No, my darling."
"She just wanted to exist," my grandfather replied.

I realized then that with each visit,
she was creating a possible version of herself.
A possible woman, a possible family.
A possible life.

SHARING.

If you share it,
it gets bigger.
Sage words of advice
that fell on unconvinced ears.

If we share too much
with others,
will we be able to support ourselves
and the ones we love?

Standing up for what is right
puts us on the firing line.
Speaking up for those without voices
opens us up for attack.

We fear we'll lose it all
if we give away too much,
which blinds us
to the obvious truth.

Let us not reach our final days
only to discover that all of the dust-covered blessings
we hoarded and hid from others
could have been shared and multiplied.

So live not with fear of losing something,
for today may be our last.
Let us spread our wings around
our fellow man, woman, beast, and plant.

Each gift we give,
be it time, money, or sweat,
will be an eternal investment
that repays itself again and again and again.

If you trust that tomorrow
the sun will rise in the east,
then have faith
that sharing love, yields love.

So cast fear aside
and let love, light, and compassion
direct your life
from this day until your last.

LONELINESS.

Loneliness is my favorite curse.
I have craved camaraderie all my life,
yet I find more profound joy in being alone,
and this condition has left me questioning.

Was I forced into solitude as a child,
or was it born within me?
What is the bland taste of groups
that leaves me drained and unfulfilled?

If I have to be among others,
give me one, not five.
For I can converse more deeply with one
than with the shallow twittering of many.

Left alone with my thoughts,
I am more than content to swim in and out
of conversations with myself
and the greater consciousness.

My emotions and musings
rise easier and more readily,
and I feel a deeper connection
to all that surrounds me. All that *is*.

Is this why I dove so aggressively
into the arms of grape and grain,
in order to dull my distaste
and to play the lovable public inebriate?

Now clear and present in head and heart,
I self-testify honestly
and allow myself to be left alone,
despite society's aversion to seclusion.

Yet here I am, alone and happy,
save for the loving company of my wife and sons.
I write and I think and I pray.
And I *thrive.*

HEART WHISPERS.

Some call it gut feeling;
others call it heart,
or guide, or perhaps the leading hand
of someone sitting on high.
Whatever name it is given,
it is a muscle,
and like any sinew,
it needs trust and practice.

It is the voice of grace
or the angel on one's shoulder,
guiding us to choose
one road above another.

It is the artistic vision
calling us to create
something from nothing.
A beautiful *David*, from a dull rock.

There is no science to prove
one way or the other.
It is simply a whisper or a nudge
or a calling from our own higher self.

It is the thing that knows
our true calling,
that pulls us back
from veering too far off track.

At times we try to ignore its call
and drown it with bottles
or grapes covered in wrath,
smothering its distant cry.

But it always remains,
summoning us to our dharma.
Even when all hope seems lost,
its faint murmur is there waiting for recognition.

So rejoice when you finally acknowledge its message,
for its voice will multiply, shaking the heavens!
With inner and outer intentions conjoined,
our destiny awaits us with jubilant arms!

CATALYST.

We are given enemies
to battle and conquer,
troubles to overcome,
and fears to vanquish.

Deprived of love,
we strive to give love to many.
Starved of food,
we vow never to go hungry again.

Is it necessary to have struggles?
Can one's potential be fulfilled
without tasting the bitterness
that will drive us forward?

The pain becomes a catalyst.
The sorrow fuels us,
and that which we think we lack
gives birth to our greatest riches.

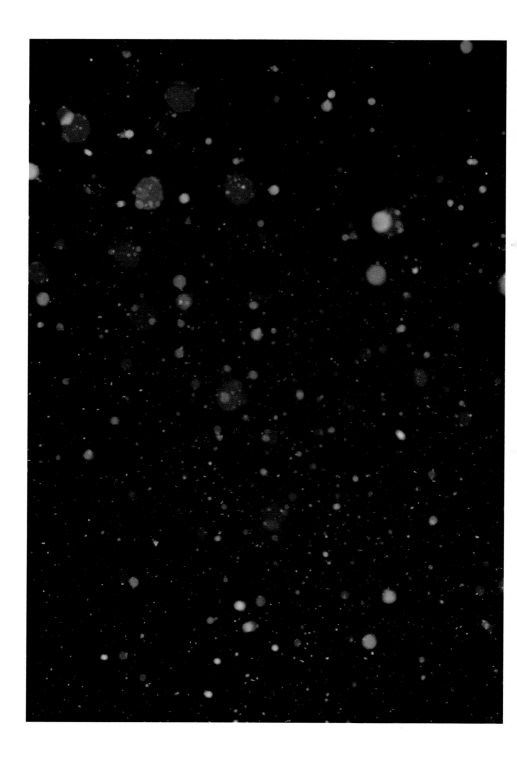

VOYAGER ONE.

Cold and alone, she flies,
traveling faster than anyone before her,
through the endless dark voids
between stars young and old.

Courageous little one,
no larger than a school bus,
whose only intention is to learn and transmit news.
Yet with no one to answer or provide comfort.

Solitary, she drifts
farther from us, her creators,
sending dispatches so faint
that we barely know she still exists.

There will be no hero's return,
no ticker-tape parade, no accolade.
For hers is the ultimate sacrifice.
Her life, for the proof of ours.

Her planetary expedition completed,
she turns her nose outward
to the unknown and untouched.
Each second, she becomes the first of us there.

She carries in her cargo of golden items
sights and sounds of our civilization.
Proving that we existed
in our small corner of this vast universe.

A greeting, or perhaps an SOS.
A message in a bottle
cast into an eternal ocean,
with no port of arrival yet known.

Her initial duty fulfilled,
she now carries this world's banner,
heading blindly into the long, dark night,
seeking someone to find her, and therefore us.

Unravaged by wind or rain,
she and her message will be preserved
for a billion years,
long after her parents die out with their sun.

She will then be
just a faint echo of our once *civilized* world,
to be heard or not heard
by someone, anyone, or no one.

She is the bravest of us
and the weakest of us,
and she will carry within her
the dreams of us all, until her dying breath.

PRAYER.

I close my eyes, and I talk to God.
I talk to my ancestors and guardians and angels.
I talk to those who are no longer here, who touched my life,
and I thank them for my many blessings.

I thank them for my eyes,
that I may see the beauty of this world.
I thank them for my ears,
which permit me to hear my loved ones' voices.

I thank them for my health
and for the miracle of today.
I thank them for showing me the way
when I am lost and alone.

I thank them for all the opportunities
that I have been given.
I thank them for the knowledge
that everything is exactly as it should be.

I surrender to them, my mind, body, and spirit,
to use as an instrument
for my most beneficial outcome,
that I may serve the good of all.

I pray that I can bring light, love, and compassion
to those around me.
I pray that I leave this world
more spiritually evolved than when I entered it.

God give me courage, wisdom, and patience.
Courage that I may stand up for what is right,
wisdom that I may know when to speak and when to listen,
and patience to be a good father and husband.

Thank you for all that you do.

But Learn, I Did

Poems of Change and Renewal

TWO YEARS SINCE YOU LEFT.

Today was the first day
that I did not long for you.
Two years to the day,
since you last touched my lips.

Ours was an intense love affair,
and you brought out the best in me.
With you I felt loved,
and I was able to love in return.

Friends at first,
we grew to adore one another.
Others would see our bond
and were warmed by our love.

You taught me to dance,
to kiss, to make love.
You made me fearless and courageous
all at once.

The perfect pair,
the life of the party.
But our need for each other
outgrew our once naïve love.

I would start to panic
if you were late to a dinner,
and people would notice
the other side of me, before you arrived.

I was split in two.
One half with you, always shining,
the other without you,
morose, insecure, and dark.

The moment you arrived,
my mood would switch
from sullen to joyful,
with an eerie air of desperation.

Once happy, all was forgiven.
We danced, joked, and feted.
Until one day something changed in me,
and it all came to a shuddering halt.

I craved independence
from your siren's call,
wanting, instead, to practice self-love
rather than the dance of fatal attraction.

Our divorce was so sudden, so harsh,
that I was unable to go out,
lest I should run into you
and fall back into your seductive arms.

In the company of others,
your absence was akin to a lack of oxygen.
Making my excuses, I would return
to the safety of my hermit existence.

Time passed,
and in place of you,
I channeled my love into
creativity and the love of others.

I found peace in stillness
and rode the high
of creative waves
and clarity of vision.

So here I sit, surrounded by people
who can love you in moderation.
And I am two years happy,
And I am two years *sober*.

CHANGE MUST COME.

What is this restlessness I feel?
Like an autumnal leaf, waiting to fall,
knowing that I am one with the tree
and knowing I will soon feed the earth below.

I feel the change that must now come to pass,
feel the cosmic continuity in which we live.
We are but raindrops in a raging river,
each of us forever evolving within a larger oneness.

So how can a single drop of water make effective change?
Are we powerless atoms within an infinite universe,
slaves to a greater plan,
or helpless leaves on a mighty oak?

Can each of us make a difference?
Cannot an atom give birth to a galaxy,
or a slave change the fortune of future generations?
Does not each leaf end up nourishing its lofty parent?

This is the change that I feel within.
Today, I will be the raindrop, and I will be the atom.
Today, I will be the seed that gives birth
to the forest of everlasting change.

PAIN AND SORROW.

Dark clouds ambush me,
snuffing the last spark
of light
from my sky.

The weight in my heart
pulls at joint and sinew,
bending my eyes toward the earth,
trailed despairingly by my head.

A distress call is echoed
to the outer limits of my aching body,
curling my neck and shoulders inward,
encasing my chest.

My stomach is laden with rocks,
every breath fighting
with the painful shallowness
of the lungs' pull.

Head, ribs, arms, and legs
all succumb
as my heart sounds the retreat,
rendering me coiled and fetal on the floor.

And here I lie.
All bodily outposts
encircling the wounded source,
protecting it in its weakened state.

And here I lie,
waiting for this shattered heart
to find its pieces
and put right what once was wrong.

Only then can my wings unfurl,
my body straighten and my head lift,
to stand tall
and take that first step, once again.

I HAVE LOST YOU.

I have lost you . . .
yet I cannot bear
to admit it to myself,
nor do I want to.

I seem to float
from room to room,
careful to avert my eyes
from any sign of you.

Picture frames, discarded clothes,
a note written by your hand.
Objects that I cannot regard
and yet cannot be moved.

For to move them
would be to shatter the fragile veneer
that separates me from reality,
and my life would surely crumble.

So I exist in denial,
like a modern-day Miss Havisham,
forever living in that last moment
of happiness that I ever knew.

Perhaps hoping that
if I stay in that frozen second,
time will one day restart
and things will be as they were.

So I wait and I avoid.
I deny and I subvert.
Until one day, I look up
and I know.

You are gone,
and I must start anew. . . .

MEDITATION.

My car had been running on fumes
for most of my life.

There were brief respites at night,
like buying a dime bag of gas.
Just enough to get me
to the next station.

I remember my life before.
Spiritually and mentally surviving from hand to mouth.
Never venturing below the shallowest surface,
preferring instead the hills and valleys of grape and green.

Then, a few years thence,
a spiritual dime bag of gas
was increased to a dollar, then five, then ten.
My life became a more profound journey,
rather than a rapid succession of pitstops.

Now able to make longer, more eloquent journeys,
I experience life through a different lens.
I soak in each vista and bathe in each minute,
with a newer, deeper connection.

ALL IS GONE.

I could tell from her face
as she made her way through
the aptly named weeping willows,
that something had changed. Something was unbalanced.

Drunk with fear, I quickened my pace to meet her.
Slipping on the dew-soaked fallen leaves,
I naïvely told myself that if I reached her soon enough,
I could somehow head off the impending annihilation of my happiness.

We finally met under the balcony,
and with an uneasy fervor, I moved to embrace her.
Her reaction was like a blunt, rusty dagger to my gut
that she twisted and twisted and twisted some more.

I could feel my insides fold inward, like an imploding star,
but I had to hide it. I had to feign strength to change her mind.
I smiled and pulled back, hoping to reel her back to me,
but she just looked down, through the ground,
to some dark and empty place.

Panicking, I pulled her waist toward me
and fiercely whispered those words,
that only yesterday made her look at me with such longing and lust.
Instead her eyes looked south with nothing behind them.
No depth. No love. No color. Just death and desolation.

Breathless, I watched my future,
seemingly so perfect just moments ago,
turn to ash and blow in a thousand directions,
leaving me undone, hollow, and forever changed.

FOG COUNTRY.

I lived in fog country
and knew nothing different.
My fog was self-made and self-inflicted,
and I found comfort in my diminished view.

The moist air clouding my vision
allowed me to see only enough to survive,
not enough to thrive.
What I couldn't see, I couldn't want.

And so I wandered through life
never knowing that mere feet away from me
hung the ripe, bursting, and succulent fruits of life,
waiting for me to seize them.

But I did not, because I saw not.
And the years passed,
and life tried to teach
a slow learner.

But learn, I did.
Meditation cleared my inner vision,
and plants replaced beasts,
cleansing my body with compassion.

A new being, I stride through the orchard of life
between branches, weighed down in blessings,
thoughts, ideas, inspiration, and love.
I stop and I see and I smile and I scize!

PEBBLES IN THE STREAM.

I look back with twenty-twenty vision,
understanding now
how those small random acts of kindness
were such defining moments in my life.

A kind word, a listening ear.
A token gesture, meaningless to the giver
but instrumental for me.
I shudder to think of the chaos of it all.

She had given me my first pencil and paper.
He had pushed me into the arts.
What if they had not been placed in my path?
What if our minutes had not coincided?

What face is given to the composer
of this complex symphony,
where note after note
appears with such apparent ease?

I wander further down this pensive pathway
glowing with gratitude
for each person of consequence,
hoping that I, too, can pass on such good fortune.

I FEEL MYSELF GETTING LOST.

I feel myself slipping.
I sense the boredom approaching
for which I used alcohol to travel through.
It scares and disappoints me at the same time.

My sons are getting older
and no longer need me
the way they did before.
I find myself sitting on the sidelines and watching.

I know I was using them as a crutch.
They were my alcohol for the last seven years.
I was allowed to overdose on my daddy duties,
and I reveled in that fact.

Now they are playing with others their age.
Now they are more independent.
I am more of a referee rather than a team player.
My duties have been diminished. I am demoted.

I am only needed to break up a fight,
find a lost ball, fix a broken toy.
I have gone from being star quarterback
to the guy who cleans the locker room.

As an addict, this is terrifying.
I suddenly have spare time, but not really.
One is still needed to be on hand,
but not needed to play the game.

I feel like a jealous lover
who has been shelved for another.
But I still have to live in the same house,
and I still have to be on call.

So that old voice comes back from the depths.
Have a drink. Relax. You deserve it.

So I have a drink.
The sips turn into gulps
because, *What the hell, I am not working tomorrow.*
I start to miss my meditations in the morning.

I notice the difference in my body.
I feel lazier and slower and emotionally heavier.
I miss being needed.
I miss the heroic abstinence because, *The kids need me to be at my best.*

And so I go from wine to straight vodka,
making up some bullshit excuse that it's better for you,
or it's cleaner, or there's less hangover,
or I drink less because it's neat.

Again, the sips gradually turn into gulps.
My immune system starts to remember the *good ole days*
where I could drink with the best of them.
My heart sinks at the memory.

My head fills itself with the lies that we tell ourselves,
and all my spiritual cleanliness and focus
is drowned out by those damned excuses.
Those excuses we know are bullshit.

I need to fill my time.
I need to regroup.
I need to quit before moderation
becomes obliteration.

But that voice keeps talking.
You know you have to take it to an extreme before you change, right?
So I try to think about flipping my compass
and heading for the other extreme of clean, soulful inebriation.

I am scared to finish this verse,
because it will be the last one today.
And that means I will have to go downstairs
and have a drink.

Let All Unsaid Things Be Said

Poems of Life and Death

I WILL DIE SOON.

I lie here with the knowledge
that the next few days will be my last.

I am dizzy with emotions that flow through me,
bitterness taking the lead,
as I feel my life being pried from my fingers.

I start to drown in the pain,
before a sudden moment of clarity is thrown to my rescue.
A breath. And then another.
A slow, calming breeze starts to disperse the anger from my mind.

Opening my eyes, I reminisce.
I recall my children and the joyful times spent together.
I hear the laughter, the love, and the moments of just *being*.
Again I breathe deeply, as lightness replaces the dark.

The radiant wind rises as gratitude flows over me.
Gratitude that I experienced
the sweetness of falling in love again,
as I was introduced to my grandchildren.

Gratitude that I was given these moments to say farewell
and that life had not been stolen
in a cruel, unplanned instant.

Even as life shuts down,
piece by piece in this shell of mine,
I hear life existing around me.

I hear my children joyfully recounting memories of us all.
I feel the touch of my grandson,
stroking my hand and kissing my cheek.

One by one, my children say everything
we always wished to say.
They speak to me of love,
and of thanks, and of peace.

Thank you, God, for these gifts.
Thank you for this precious time together.

I feel the final chambers in my body
closing up shop,
and my family gathers,
to clothe me in love before I leave.

I take my final breath of this life,
in the same manner that I took my first,
my eyes closed, with a fear of the unknown,
and carrying with me nothing but my soul.

I remain in the room, but I feel no pain.
I see my wife and children
cradling my head and hands in theirs.
Tears fall as they embrace my discarded armor.

Gradually I feel part of something larger,
something grander, something greater.

No longer bound by earthly constraints,
I feel myself everywhere all at once.

I place my hand on my loved ones' shoulders.
Do not cry, I whisper. *I will be with you, always.*

TALK TO ME ALWAYS.

Do not stop conversing with me
after I am gone.

For the physical body
may have left your sight,
but I will always be beside you.

Do not think that I have departed
or withdrawn from you.
For I am more with you now
than I ever was before.

I am traveling with you,
above and beyond you.
I feel your thoughts,
and I hear your prayers.

I am here.

Speak my name,
and I am here.
Call for help,
and I am here.

Ready to celebrate
when you are jubilant,
and close with comforting arms
when you are wounded in heart or head.

I am here.

You know my voice.
So do not despair
if you do not hear me reply,
for your heart hears me as clear as day.

I am here.

More able and more present, I am with you.
Physical laws can no longer confine me,
and I transcend all dimensions
within you and without you.

I am here.

Close your eyes.
See my face smiling back at you.
Rest your head on my shoulder
and know that I will be with you, *always.*

MY STEPFATHER'S PASSING.

Like moths encircling a dimming flame,
we hang on your every breath, every murmur.

Your ancestors start to gather.

Your body, weathered by internal tempests and struggle,
does not mirror your soul's peaceful beauty,
soon to be unveiled in a heavenly celebration.

You are close now.

Let all unsaid things be said!
Let us whisper of love, of thanks, and of happiness.
Take flight with full knowledge
of your loving and beloved legacy!

Slowly, your earthly shackles loosen
as you draw your last breath.

We pray for help releasing your vessel,
knowing that your spirit will be with us always.
It is time for your wings to unfurl
as you bathe in eternal light.

You are loved.
Go in peace.

You are loved.

WAVE FIGHTER.

I wade arrogantly into the spray
like an overconfident fighter,
puffing out my chest
as if to goad this unknown opponent.

As soon as the bell rings, a haymaker lands on my jaw,
and salted naïvety drains from my nose.
I get straight up and smirk it off.
"Sucker punch," I mutter, as I shake off the foam.

Ignoring cautious instincts,
I sidestep one punch and jab through another.
I turn again and am immediately pummeled with an uppercut.
Momentarily stunned, I have no time to rebound.

A right, then a left. I lower my head to face him head-on.
I swing blindly while trying to wipe his spit from my eyes.
Either he is growing with each punch
or, pound for pound, I am out of my depth.

Yet there is fight left in this brawler yet.
I weave, I dodge, and glance up beyond my sodden fists.
Doubled in size, he suddenly towers above me,
and I see certain annihilation about to descend.

Instinct takes over, and I dive, kicking furiously to escape the avalanche.
Under him, I feel the weight of his punch
as it crashes like a demolished building
onto my feet, before they slip through to freedom.

I propel myself up and gratefully gasp for air,
but he is not done, not by a long shot.
The first being a decoy, he thunders all of his fury down,
and I am out. Gone. Decimated.

Round, down, and twisted I go, like a limp and torn ragdoll,
not knowing my up from my down, left from my right.
I try to find air, but he pulls my legs down,
determined to drown all arrogance from my lungs.

I feel the ground for a split second and push off.
Finding air, I breathe in with a wild roar of desperation.
Punch drunk and pride stung, I spin around.
"Is that all you've got?" I scream.

He laps gently at my legs, grins, and retreats.
Out for the count, my knees give way.
And I find myself slumped in the shallows,
spitting out salt and thanking the referee upstairs that I am alive.

No more. You win.

IF I DO NOT RETURN.

If I don't come home today,
there are things that I need you all to know.

Know that my life had meaning because of you.
You gave me purpose and goals,
to be a better husband, father, and person,
to protect and guide you.

Know that I will always be with you.
Even if I am not here in body,
my spirit will be but a heartbeat away,
loving you and bathing you in light.

Know that you can always speak to me.
Just whisper my name, and I will be there
with an understanding ear and nurturing heart.
You will *never* be alone.

Know that you have painted my life with joy.
From the moment our eyes met,
my world was filled with color,
and each dawn broke with a life-affirming smile.

Know that you all fill me with boundless pride.
Your nature is that of love and of compassion,
and this world is all the more wealthy
for having you in it.

Know that your names commence my prayers.
Know that you *will* be OK.
Know that I will never leave your sides.
Know that my arms are waiting for you, always.

FINAL CALL.

I discovered recently
that I am going to die,
and everything was body-slammed
into perspective.

Suddenly I realized
that my time to live fully
and to do good
was finite.

Bitterness and anger were swatted away
with the hand of blind courage,
leaving no time to care
for others' opinions of my new outlook.

My goal now,
is to effect as much
positive change as possible
in my short time left.

I will spend my last few days loving my family,
laughing easily at life,
and working to leave a legacy
of love and light and compassion.

All those clichés of deathbed regrets
will not be mine.
I have been given my final notice,
and I will not squander another minute.

I will sing, I will write,
I will speak from my heart when I feel it,
through love-soaked poems,
and I will not slink quietly into the night.

Every day counts; every minute matters.
I will offer my hand in help while I am still able,
and I will stand up for others
while I still have these strong legs to carry me.

I will seize every opportunity
given to me from the heavens,
turning away fear at the door,
for this is my time!

And when and how will I die?

Hopefully, when I am one hundred years of age,
smiling, surrounded by loved ones.
But I will die. That is for sure.
So now I choose to live.

A BANNER TO RAISE.

I now know what I have to do.
What confused me as a youth
and frustrated me as a young adult
is now as clear as day.

Born in modern times but with blood stained blue.
Two sides of life, both forced upon me.
One life of duty, history, and loss.
The other of a contemporary player.

Like any youth, I felt different,
a feeling of not belonging
due to geographical movements
or from a different sense of purpose.

The more I learned of my history,
the more confused I became,
since the past and the present
would never marry for me.

So I reject it all,
preferring to live in the *now,* rather than the *then.*
And I exist like those around me,
happy to unload the burden of the past.

But now I hold in my arms a son
who shares the same lineage as I.
What will he know? How will he live?
I am forced to see my life anew.

My past is not a weight to carry,
but a banner to raise.
No longer a burden of duty,
but a standard to live by.

As my ancestors fought and forged new lives,
so shall I raise the name of my bloodline
in pursuit of charity, chivalry, and leadership,
with my weapons of love and compassion.

Let me show you, my son,
the best man that I can be.
Let my legacy to you be one of a man evolved,
so that you, too, can find your way in this world.

THREE YOUNG MEN.

Three young men,
each hailing from different lives and lands,
thrown together
into the trenches of life.

In another life,
we would have met and parted ways
with pleasantries and smiles,
never to meet again.

Differing backgrounds,
that brought varying experiences,
now forced to live in close quarters
and exist together.

After weeks, our true selves appear,
no longer able to hold up
each other's false facades.
No longer able to sustain the pretense.

We see the best of each other.
We see the worst of each other.
Our strengths and weaknesses
battling side by side for all to see.

Now we three strangers, bonded by shared encounters,
find ourselves together on a foundation of
raw honesty, life, love, and laughter.
And for them, I am grateful.

Live with Purpose,
Love All, and Harbor No Regrets

Poems of Courage

GREAT IS THE ONE.

Great are they
who are able to change,
for they hold the bounty of the world
on the tips of their fingers.

Easier is the path
of tradition and familiarity,
when all that we have acquired
has come from them.

But bravely, instead we choose
to ride the crest of a new wave
and renew ourselves
over and over again.

We choose to lead by example
and change minds of others like us,
knowing that our new journey
will leave a wake of hope and compassion.

We will not look backward
and question our choices,
for we have eyes fixed ahead,
proud of what we will become.

So, great are they
who choose to evolve and change,
for they know that each moment
is a chance for eternal rebirth.

WOULD YOU SPEND YOUR LIFE?

I recall releasing my first poem into the world.
Midnight, I lay awake, tormented by fear.
Fear of failure, sneering voices,
mockery, or disapproval.

Should I retract it?
Will people think me a fool,
over-amorous, or a hack?
How dare I venture outside my wheelhouse?

Then a voice came to me.

Would you spend your life
whispering your love in her ear,
or would you rather look back
having roared it from a mountaintop, from time to time?

And I smiled.

And I slept.

SON OF A FALLEN MAN.

Son of a fallen man,
betrayed by his brother.

How could I have known
my life would end this way.

To be born into the bondage of revenge.
To be held prisoner by rage.

How can I avenge my lineage
if I choose the path that is right?

How can I look my father in the face
when all is said and done?

If I take the higher road,
I fail my lifelong mission.

This mission that sustained me when I was weak
and nourished me when I was close to death.

This poison that flows through my veins
is the very glue that holds my broken pieces together.

So I am lost.
I hold the keys
and yet am unable to free myself
from my own sentence.

RETRIBUTION.

"I can make you or break you," he half joked
as he stood over her before she went on stage.
She winced as she smelled the stale cherry perfume
that had rubbed off on him from one of his recent "auditions."

Those poor girls, just looking for a chance,
and these loathsome men who sweat over them
like the overweight gluttons that they are,
promising anything to get to their dessert.

They dangled fame and fortune in front of them
and made them bet away their self-worth,
never knowing whether they should draw the line
or if *one more minute* would actually mean their big break.

He leaned closer and wheezed a more sordid threat.
She feigned apathy, raised one penciled eyebrow and smirked.
She could see the anger boiling underneath his left eye,
and a bead of sweat rolling over some poorly erased lipstick.

They heard the crowd applaud again
as the penultimate act came to a close.
She tried to reapply her lipstick, just to give herself something to do,
but her trembling hands gave away her true state.

She stood up and walked toward stage left,
ignoring the threatening grumblings of the man behind her.
Did he know what she was about to do?
Would he have stopped her, killed her, if he had known?

It didn't matter now. This was her retribution.
This was for that night when he had used her dreams against her.
This was for all the girls yet to have his reality thrust in their face.
The curtains open, and she raises her eyes to the audience.

"Ladies and gentlemen, I would like to tell you a tale. . . ."

EMBRACING MY YOUNGER SELF.

From time to time
I see my infant self,
my teenage self,
my vulnerable self.

I realize that I live my life
in a constant crusade
to protect the younger me
by strengthening the elder.

Sent away against my will,
beaten into submission
by loneliness and longing for a tender ear
and protecting arms.

Toughened and alone,
I learned to trust only myself,
relying on no others
for my happiness or sense of well-being.

Now, a parent
with young of my own,
I do everything in my power
to instill security and love.

By guarding them
from isolation and pain,
I comfort the innocent youth in me,
promising that all will end well.

LIVING WITHOUT FEAR.

You blessed me with
your departing wisdom,
as we conversed
during your final days.

You gave me the gift
of future hindsight,
and with that,
I now direct my life.

I no longer fear
the disapproval or judgment of others,
for I recognize that my goal
is to love and evolve.

I know that this sprint called life
will only be won
if I run my own race
and believe in a higher intention.

So I thank you for teaching me,
in your own unique way,
how to live with purpose,
love all, and harbor no regrets.

THURSDAY'S CHILD.

Defeated and slouched over my legs, I sit.
Dark clouds atop my fallen head,
tinged black with the ash of
scorched rainforests and corrupt rulers.

Try as I might to see any hope,
the enormity of our demise looms,
and I watch in despair
as my children, my descendants, innocently play.

Daily, we try to stem the tsunami
of our polluted and poisoned neglect,
yet we are outweighed and outgunned
by the armies of avarice and greed.

Those armies who are blind
to their own downfall,
not realizing that with each gluttonous act,
they pull our world closer to the precipice.

I see those around me,
struck dumb by these unbeatable foes,
unable to lift their sword,
unable to see any sign of a war being won.

Thursday's Child then whispers to me.
He tells me that it is not our war to win.
We fight these bloodied skirmishes,
that our *descendants* may one day taste victory.

So let not frustration dull your blade,
for each small stone we lay,
will be the foundation from which generations yet unborn
will rise high, over evil.

The King in his wisdom,
knew that he would not see the Promised Land,
yet his reign allowed his followers
to reach it in his stead.

So raise your head once more!
Lead, fight, and inspire.
For the battle for our survival is at hand,
and we cannot and we must not fail.

EXCITING TIMES.

We live in exciting times
where real change is possible,
where technology can teach us
what is happening at home and away.

So if we do not know about
the suffering of others,
it is not for lack of knowledge,
but for lack of a desire to know.

In decades past, we could turn away blindly
and wait for others to change first.
We could blame the machine
for being too big to adapt.

But we are the parts
that make up the machine.
We have the information in our pockets;
we just need to click and proceed.

We exist in a fortunate age,
where the research has been done
and the direction is clear.
We must simply take the first step.

So let us grab the chance
that has been handed us.
Let us ride the wave of the pioneers
who paved the way before us.

How blessed is our generation,
to have the knowledge, tools,
necessity, and opportunity
to make real and effective change.

The time is at hand,
and the demand is deafening.
Let us stand up for what is right
and inspire all to join us on this quest.

Tomorrow Does Not Exist, and Yesterday Is All But Forgotten

Poems of Memory and Time

THINKING OF YOU.

Whenever I'm in nature, I think of you.
Wishing you were by my side,
recognizing each faint bird call
or the turning colors of the trees.

Memories of a porch in Africa,
the distinct flavor of your cigarette hanging in the warm, dry evening air
as we counted the falling stars,
blazing theatrically against the inky black sky.

A fog-laden Oxford morn,
with icy dew covering the land.
Your boots crunching on the frosted driveway.
The damp smell of your wax-coated jacket.

The Sunday smell of cut grass. The moth-eaten sweaters.
The sudden eyebrow raise, at the owl's call.
Saluting the magpies. One for sorrow, two for joy.
Moments that seemed irrelevant then, and now so deeply missed.

Now a father, I walk out into *my* country night.
I look up into the star-speckled sky and feel the emptiness next to me.
I sit silently in the garden, as you once did, and listen,
wishing I had stayed longer, with you, all those times.

Each morning, I walk my son around the garden and converse with you.
I comment on the falling leaves, the ancient trees,
the silence in the air, and I ask my son if a deer will grace us.
Only you would be as excited, as I now am.

The simplicity of your requests shames me.
"Come outside and listen to this."
"Have you seen the light outside . . . ?"
Requests declined with an adolescent shrug.

To my dismay, you never saw my home, but I feel you here.
With each snowfall or passing beast,
there you are, by my side, eyebrows twitching,
giving voices and personae to each sound.

Dear John, I miss you and your gentle soul.
I thank you for all those simple yet beautiful moments,
and I pray I can do the same for my sons,
with you by my side.

OLD HOME MOVIE.

The old home movie
flickers into life,
as the guitar melody
plucks at my heart strings.

Faces much younger than today beam with light,
free from care or worry,
sun kissed and lightly salted
from Aphrodite's emerald sea.

We dive from rock faces
into the crystal depths,
where we glide and float
with childlike glee.

She turns and laughs at the camera,
and my breath is halted
as it was on that very day.
Such remains her spell over me.

The boat rocks to and fro
around the reclined Goddess of Love,
and we slip off the bow
to steal tender interludes in her hidden caves.

Spent on deck, her head rests on my beating chest
as our *Argo* rocks gently,
hiding and revealing the setting sun
with each passing undulation.

We deliciously doze and kiss salty lips,
before the old man and the sea
herald our return voyage,
around this mythical rock.

As the movie reaches its final act,
she walks toward the day-weary sun,
turns, and sweetly smiles,
stopping even the guitar's strings in their tracks.

This was ten years ago,
and still those heavenly notes float through me,
ripening and swelling my heart like a peach,
and I am sweetened once more.

JET LAG.

Three thirty-seven a.m. blinks at me
from the table clock;
sleep has eluded me
for the last hour and a half.

I sit up in my silent hotel room,
so deathly quiet I can hear the sockets hum.
The battle to sleep has been fought and lost
and I, the vanquished, am alone with my thoughts.

I used to fear these moments
of unbroken contemplation,
always wishing to drown them out
with aural and visual distractions.

But now I feel peace.
I can swim in the undisturbed
tide pools of my mind,
allowing memories and wishes to wash over me.

I wonder why I avoided these moments
with such passion,
as if I would drown in the onslaught of regret,
shame, or wishes unfulfilled.

I listen to the void, shut my eyes,
and converse with myself.
No longer afraid of what may unravel,
for I know that I can only leave enriched.

These are the moments of magic,
when no one and no thing
can disturb my direct line
to the source and its knowledge.

In a few hours,
dawn will let loose the hounds of daily life,
and other people's existence
will storm the walls of my fort of tranquility.

So I sit and harvest all that I can
from these fields of meditative reflection
as I clothe myself in gratitude
for the coming day.

LAST EVIDENCE OF JOY.

An old photograph falls from a book,
and I see them young and free from the burdens of life.

I barely recognize her smile, so innocent and carefree.
There are no lines left by the life battles yet to come.

Her future is open, full of potential and promise,
knowing nothing of what is to befall her.

And him. That game smile and those devilish eyebrows.
He is an easy read once you know
what the last page of the book looks like.

I remember that car of his. They were married beside it,
on the side of the road in some sleepy New Mexico town.

She couldn't have known. She was too naïve and trusted everyone.
He could have convinced her to walk through fire, such was his way.

I would have warned her, if I were more of a man,
but something inside me wanted her to do it. I wanted to teach her.

She couldn't have known, could she?
Or was there more to her than she let on?

Was that innocent light that I saw in her eyes
simply a veil to disguise her self-destructive nature?

Either way, the photograph was the last evidence of joy in her life.
The last known document of peace, before war was declared.

NYC DAWN.

They say it is always darkest
the moment before the dawn.
Well, that moment has just passed,
and light has found a way to creep back in.

I walk down Sixth Avenue, bathed in a bluish-green hue,
in what seems like a postapocalyptic street scene.
Garbage is strewn across the street
like cadavers from the previous night's battle.

The stale stench of alcohol
and a distinct saccharin odor from everything
that is overproduced in this world
hangs like death in the early morning mist.

I sidestep a few *walking dead*
who stumble toward me on the sidewalk,
and I find myself alone,
walking in the middle of the avenue.

My vision is uninterrupted all the way up to the fifties
as I walk up the spine
of this concrete canyon,
feeling like the lone survivor of a global catastrophe.

I stop midblock, close my eyes, and listen.
The emptiness is chilling.
I know that in less than an hour, this will be the busiest
and most exciting city in the world.

I conclude that this concrete giant,
the home of millions, must also sleep.
The faint snoring of the early subway trains underfoot
is the only sound of this slumbering beast.

Without the usual noise and visual distractions,
the concrete titans that loom above me,
cast in sweat, steel, and rock,
seem taller and more powerful than usual.

My neck cranes to see the top of these wardens,
and I sense them leaning over
to inspect this small intruder
venturing through their arteries.

These giants were created by titans who rule the city.
They can raise or crush you,
shoot you to the stars, or bury you for one misstep.
Here, in order to survive, you have to walk tall and think taller.

All at once, the tallest few of the mythical creatures
turn toward the east
and their faces glow
in the reflected glory of the sun god.

A taxi's howl awakens me from my pensive interlude,
and the city leaps into life as if it had never slept. . . .
"Get outtah the road, asshole!"

Ah . . . I love you, too, New York!

BIRD WATCHING.

Day after day, I watched her
from my father's bedroom.
She was never late, never underdressed,
and she never, ever spoke.

Like clockwork, at 5 p.m.,
I would regard this elegant beauty
as she descended from her shadowed balcony
to the beach below.

No one knew anything about her,
so they assumed
she was a widower, a scorned lover,
or an orphaned heiress.

I myself surmised
that she dressed older than her young age.
Her skin was perfectly taught,
and her neck resembled that of a swan.

I imagined stories—a gifted ballerina,
career cut short by a tragedy of some sort.
Maybe she had been left at the altar?
A younger, more beautiful Miss Havisham.

On my sixteenth birthday,
I was given binoculars to watch the birds.
I naturally ignored every feathered visitor,
opting to study this enigmatic flamingo instead.

I zoomed in closer
and saw, for the first time, evidence of tears
that left a telling track
through her generously applied face powder.

She had small burn marks on her fingers.
Evidence of her cigarettes
burning down to the base
while she stood, hypnotized by the horizon.

I desperately wanted to know more.
Who was she? Where was she from?
What was her history?
What caused her pain?

But just as I was a prisoner of my house,
so, too, was she a prisoner of her own story,
That is, until the morning
after my father's funeral . . .

EVEN LOVE SONGS DIE.

How can one write a love story,
that will last longer
than the flickering light
of its short life in eternity?

We fear our love will cease to exist
once we are no longer alive
to fan the flames
that meld us together.

So we create songs, poems, and art
with metaphors, imagery, and color,
hoping to immortalize and give credence to our love,
hoping that this tells our story for all time.

If the story outlives us,
then our love has a chance to survive,
to inspire art, touch people's souls,
and allow them to taste our devotion on their lips.

But even love songs are destined to die.
The winds of time inevitably
blow away the embers of any love,
no matter how high the flames burned.

We and our love
will leave to feed the cosmic heart
that vibrates through us all,
nurturing the true *one love* that is eternal.

ATTIC.

I enter my old room in the attic,
and with each step on the old wooden floor,
thirty years of undisturbed dust shudders
and rises slowly into the air.

I walk toward the small, oval window,
brush away the spider's intricate artwork,
and crack open the rusted latch
as old paint chips fall to my feet.

The fresh, warm evening air
floods into the room
like a dam that has been released.
I am reminded of how *she* used to enter my room.

My chest expands,
and I breathe in the dusk breeze,
soaked in pine trees and orange groves
from down below, where we spent most days.

I lie back onto my childhood bed
and rest my head against decaying stuffed toys,
my feet stretched out over the end,
like gargoyles hanging over a Roman ruin.

The gentle wind blowing through the window
lifts and releases the long, tattered lace curtains,
and the golden sun flutters behind.
Eyes squinted, I see her hovering before me.

She is clothed in heavenly light,
adorned with gold-trimmed wings.
Her warmth and love flowing over me,
she whispers to me that she is at peace.

As the sun's rays illuminate each floating dust particle,
thoughts of her fill my head,
and I know she is no longer here
because she is now, everywhere.

I feel her love but not as before.
No longer a love of passion and joy and pain,
but a love that encompasses all that I see,
all that I hear and feel.

She is the light.
She is the wind.
She is the dust,
and she is me.

SHE IS LATE.

She is late, *again.*
She was supposed to be here at eight,
and in anticipation, I have been ready since seven,
hovering around my front door since seven fifty-five.

Half an hour has passed
since she was supposed to knock on that door.
Every minute past eight is more uncomfortable than the last,
and my heart hovers somewhere between anger and despair.

Forty-five minutes. Sixty minutes. Ninety minutes.
I feel wounded and want to lash out by leaving.
A text arrives, and I fumble my phone from my pocket.
"Can't find a taxi anywhere," she says.

Can't find a taxi?! CAN'T FIND A TAXI?!
Why is she just now looking for a taxi?
Furious, I grab my jacket and head out the door,
but before it slams behind me, my foot reaches back to block it.

My pride pushes me to exit this painful scene,
but my newfound love for this girl holds me back.
I want to retreat, drown my petulance, and ignore her calls.
I want to teach her a lesson, but I am left completely undone.

Despite the pain this waiting inflicts on me,
I would rather wait for days
than not see her at all.
Being late is beauty's privilege, someone once said.

I hate that someone.
I hate the fact that she has this power over me.
Yet I know that every second spent with her
feels different from any spent before she came into my life.

"Take your time," I mutter under my breath.
I will brood when you arrive,
but inside I will be smiling and sighing,
knowing that I will wait for you, *always*.

OLD PHOTOGRAPHS.

I used to see her walking through the woods from time to
time.

She never looked at me, and she always seemed to be
listening for something, as if she were waiting for someone to
call her name.

She walked with no purpose or direction, as if the
slightest breeze would change her path.

I daydreamed that one day
she would turn and see me.
She would look directly into my eyes and smile,
the way I had seen her smile in old photographs.

If only I had known then what impact she would have on my
life, I would never have followed her that day.

Somewhere between This Place and That

Poems of Home and Travel

TRAVEL ALONE.

Travel alone.
Be at peace
with anxious trepidation,
for that is where the wonders lie.

Better to see the world
undiluted by a companion's familiarity.
Instead, be a silent voyeur
wandering through distant lives.

Listen not to your songs from home.
Allow every sense to be fed
by the new and unknown,
unencumbered by what you already know.

Travel with pen and paper.
Let this be your sole companion
with whom you can decipher each feeling,
each experience, nuance, exhilaration, and fear.

Voyage with your thoughts,
allowing each new vista, smell, and experience
to open the floodgates of your mind
to imagination, memories, and wishes.

Free-fall into the depths
of who you are
and who you will be,
and there, exist in the magic of life.

TICK TOCK.

Tick tock, tick tock.

I sip my coffee, laced with mother's ruin,
and try to stifle my strained breath
as I wait for my steed
to emerge from its slumber.

The second hand of my watch
slices the dawn air
like a rusty blade,
tick after labored tock.

I feign rotten complacency
and try to survive those moments before the flag drops,
those moments that can push
even the strongest men to madness.

Tick . . . tock . . .

My beast rolls off,
dust vibrating on its lid,
as the motor gurgles to life
like a waking drunkard.

Tick, goddamn tock.

Just get me behind the wheel,
so I can feel the dust hitting the creases of my face,
where nothing can touch me
and time just, stops.

CUBA'S GRANDDAUGHTER.

She glows with pride as she sets eyes on you.
Embracing you, she whispers stories of your ancestors
as her sea-born breeze gently caresses your hair.
She is proud of her granddaughter.

Long has she waited for this day. . . .
For many years she has watched you grow from afar.
A seed blown far from its native tree,
who now comes home as a parent with seed of her own.

Breathe deep, my child, she whispers.
Smell the earth of your parents and parents' parents.
With every breath, let the lives and experiences of your homeland flow through you.
Feel the spirit of Mother Cuba awaken within you.

You explore her features, somehow familiar.
The deep wrinkles in her face speak of love, life, and song.
Her smile is the daily sun rising over a shimmering sea,
and each star in the night sky mirrors the sparkle in her deep-set eyes.

Your ancestors approach to welcome their prodigal daughter.
The blood in your veins pumps faster, now closer to its source.
Strange sights, smells, and sounds stir past life memories
as your heart sings in unison with its native tongue.

In her lies the last puzzle piece needed to know yourself.
In her, you see the place from whence you came
and know she has given you the courage to travel the road before you.
She is your soul. She is you. She is Cuba.

A NEED TO BELONG.

I used to want to belong.
A gang, a people, or a country
was all I desired. To be one of many.
To be the same.

But I could not, because I was not.
A fish out of water, I was alone.
I knew of my supposed origins,
but each source nation was just a fraction of my whole.

How can you be one of the team,
when you are a team of one?
From whom can you draw strength and experience
when there seems to be no one like you?

The source of my pain and apparent weakness
gradually became my foundation and my strength
as I realized that belonging to no one
meant a freedom to belong to everyone.

No longer a sole victim,
I was now a member of the world,
drawing from many soils
and free to absorb them all.

My desire to belong was now a desire to dream bigger.
The shackles of conforming and pleasing one's people
were exchanged for the freedom to choose my own path
and engage with whomever I pleased.

The world is my home,
and its countries are my people.
I will never belong to anything smaller,
nor shall I ever wish to.

TRAVELING PARENT.

I sit on top of clouds,
somewhere between this place and that.
My thoughts tinged with gray
as I think of my family at home.

For I am a traveling parent,
taking work, wherever work takes me.
But with the adventures and wonders of journeying
also comes the burden of solitude and longing.

In the same instance,
I am so grateful for work, so grateful for travel,
and I know how fortunate I am
to see the world and its wondrous sights.

I close my eyes and give thanks for allowing me
to see the morning sun rise above the Pacific Ocean.
Yet I count the days until I will see the faces of my sons,
rising over the side of my bed.

I am blessed to hear the warm westerly wind
blowing through the African savanna,
but how I would smile to hear my sons' giggles
as they play in the kitchen while I cook.

The exhilaration of a breath-stealing vista
will always carry a heavy aftertaste,
as I cannot share it
with the woman I love.

Such is my adult existence,
to be blessed with such incredible experiences
and yet unable to share them
with those I hold dearest.

As I gaze across the China sky
from thirty thousand feet,
I vow to spend more time playing with my sons
and to shower my wife with kisses when she least expects it.

I regret not reading my boys that last bedtime story
or allowing that phone call
to disturb me bathing them.
I will do better and be better when I return.

I close my eyes,
and I see my family's faces.
I whisper that it will not be long
before we all embrace again.

FIRST HOME.

I walked around your empty space
when your bones were first forming,
trying to imagine what you would become
and where each room would be.

I walked through your finished doorway
the day after my honeymoon
with my love by my side,
ready to start a new chapter.

As a young married couple,
we grew together, loved together, and fought together.
We made up together,
and we made a nest for whomever might join us.

Do you remember that day years ago
just weeks before Christmas
when she told me she was with child,
and I screamed with joy at the news?

We walked through the elevator doors,
carefully carrying our firstborn,
placing his cot gently upon your floor
to let the dog introduce himself.

Again, we grew as one living, breathing unit,
your walls giving shelter,
and your windows giving ever-changing light
and inspiring views of this incredible city.

A few years more of love, laughter, joy, pain, and growing
before we brought our second child home.
You cradled our family as we introduced brother to brother,
none of us realizing how much this moment would mean to us.

Seasons change, and we all grew and evolved.
We fixed parts of you, and we fixed parts of ourselves.
You watched over us silently
as we nursed our boys through sleepless nights.

Strong, unshakable, protective, nurturing.
You felt our pain when we lost loved ones
and shared in our joy
as we welcomed family and friends.

You were our first home
and the birthplace
of our family's love,
and I love you for that.

HOME.

The morning chorus streams through the eastern trees,
carrying the promise of a new day.
A turn around the garden breathes fresh life into our souls.
A child's laughter, a deep sigh.

A gentle breeze dances through the twisted branches.
I stare into the sun, smiling, as the light momentarily blinds me.
Breathe deep. Thank the ancestors.
I feel the energy of life passing through me into the earth below.

You cradle us in your old arms,
silencing the clatter in our heads.
You have lived through others' lives,
felt their joy and their heartache.

Feel now our love.
Feel now our peace.
Feed off the life and family
that grows within your walls.

The setting sun dapples crimson light through trees in the west,
while blood-red leaves are gently released to feed the soil.
Father and son stop to greet each tree.
They are our hosts, we their guests.

As night falls and our eyelids begin to weigh heavy,
we are drawn in toward the heart of the home.
The family's faces glow as the fire burns,
and we nourish our hearts and souls.

As the fire subsides, we snuff out the remaining lights.
The ancestors gather as our dreams spread their wings.
Your broad shoulders brace for the cool of the night.
Until dawn breaks, the morning streams in, and we begin again.

READY TO LEAVE.

I have lived my life
always ready to leave each new place.
The bag on my back filled with all I would need,
lest I should have to depart this very night.

Every essential item I own
has always been an arm's reach away.
As a child at school
my five belongings lived next to my bed.

Each year, my parents told me
that we would soon sell up and leave.
So my mind lay in perpetual preparedness
to uproot, shift sideways, and start again.

This curse and blessing
battled within me.
I could adapt immediately,
yet I was too fearful to put down roots.

My bachelor's pad lay bare
save for my core essentials:
two cases of clothes
and eight boxes of art books.

No cushion, chair, pot, or frame
would burden my voyaging legs.
Any creature comfort would be borrowed
and left at each temporary station.

I could leave each port within the hour,
and I loved the romantic sense of freedom.
Yet still I envied others' ability
to nest and create a home.

Then you moved in,
and one day
I saw a small stone bust
sitting atop a shelf.

It did not feed,
clothe, or shelter me,
and it held no immediate purpose
that I could ascertain.

Yet through it, I heard a word
for the first time
in my adult existence.
I felt an untapped emotion called home.

The bust was soon followed by other trinkets
whose sole purpose was simply
to adorn, shine, or create
a warm hearth in our house.

And now
I have a home.
Each wall and shelf
filled with love.

Yet strangely, when alone, I find myself sitting on my bed,
bag and core essentials by my side,
ready to depart a life
I will never want to leave.

ACKNOWLEDGMENTS

My humble thanks go to:

Giada Lubomirski
John Mainwaring
Pamela Mainwaring
Ladislas Lubomirski
Anne Bohner
Patty Rice
Kathy Hilliard
Anne du Boucheron
Emily Ullrich
Alida Zimmerman

ADDITIONAL PHOTO CREDITS

Giada Lubomirski—pages 40 and 50
Pedro Alves—page 62
Pamela Mainwaring—page 60

Concern Worldwide is a nongovernmental, international, humanitarian organization dedicated to the reduction of suffering and working toward the ultimate elimination of extreme poverty in the world's poorest countries. Since its foundation in 1968, Concern Worldwide—through its work in emergencies and long-term development—has saved countless lives, relieved suffering, and provided opportunities for a better standard of living for millions of people. It works primarily in the countries ranked in the bottom forty of the United Nations' Human Development Report. Concern Worldwide implements emergency response programs as well as long-term development programs in the areas of livelihoods, health, HIV/AIDS, and education.

www.concernworldwide.org

@concernworldwideus

AUTHOR BIO

Alexi Lubomirski is a world-renowned fashion and portrait photographer who shoots celebrity cover stories for magazines such as *Vogue, Elle,* and *Harper's Bazaar* across the globe. Among other things, Lubomirski shot the official engagement and wedding portraits for Prince Harry and Ms. Meghan Markle.

In 2014, he published *Princely Advice for a Happy Life,* a book written for his two young sons, on the virtues of behaving in a manner befitting a prince in the twenty-first century. In 2019, he published a children's book, *Thank You for My Dreams: Bedtime Prayers of Gratitude,* aiming to create an occasion for children and adults to express, enjoy, and connect through their gratitude.

Lubomirski is also a global ambassador for the humanitarian charity Concern Worldwide, to which he donates all of his books' proceeds.

He lives in New York with his wife @ecoshaker and their two sons.

@alexilubomirski

INDEX

TALK TO ME ALWAYS

Andrews McMeel Publishing
a division of Andrews McMeel Universal
1130 Walnut Street, Kansas City, Missouri 64106

www.andrewsmcmeel.com

20 21 22 23 24 TEN 10 9 8 7 6 5 4 3 2 1

ISBN: 978-1-5248-5693-9

Library of Congress Control Number: 2020934527

Editor: Patty Rice
Art Director: Tiffany Meairs
Production Editor: Jasmine Lim
Production Manager: Tamara Haus

ATTENTION: SCHOOLS AND BUSINESSES

Andrews McMeel books are available at quantity discounts with
bulk purchase for educational, business, or sales promotional use.
For information, please e-mail the Andrews McMeel Publishing
Special Sales Department: specialsales@amuniversal.com.